Meal Prep

The Ultimate Meal Prep Guide

Table of Contents

Introduction

Chapter 1 – What is meal prepping?

Chapter 2 – Let's get started

Chapter 3 – Foods to Avoid and include

Chapter 4 – Useful tips and techniques

Chapter 5 – Awesome Hacks and Ideas

Chapter 6 – Delicious Recipes

Conclusion

Introduction

Every day people are looking for solutions to eat healthy. Believe me, it is never an easy task to plan meals that are not just tasty but healthy as well. However, because people have busy schedule, children to take care of, or sometimes find it hard to prepare meals – they tend to just eat what they can immediately buy or what is available in their pantry.

Not everyone has the time and budget to always prepare mouth-watering meals in a jiffy. Others, for that matter don't know how to prepare meals in advance because they find it hard to do. But remember, healthy eating has a lot great benefits that will not only be good for you, but for your whole family as well.

Congratulations for you now have the solution to your meal prepping woes! This is a great book that will help you get started in preparing nutritious meals for the whole family even if you are busy. In this book you will learn the basics of food prepping, different foods that you can use to prep your meals in a lot of different ways and more importantly teach you to prepare them the right and nutritious way!

Meal prepping is time saving, healthy and budget friendly. Aside from that it is generally a form of habit that you can include in your daily life. There's no right or wrong way on how to prep your meals, the important thing is that you accumulate the knowledge and make use of it. The possibilities and benefits are truly worthwhile.

Start reading and start prepping your meals! Have fun learning and preparing!

Chapter 1 – What is meal prepping?

When it comes to eating healthy foods, preparation is always the best key to success. One study even suggests that spending your time on cooking and preparing meals is directly linked to having better dietary habits. Meal prepping or meal prep is now becoming a popular craze all throughout the nation. They have been going mainstream and more people are now trying their hand on this kind of food preparation system. People who are engaged on special diets such as Weight Watchers or Paleo have been enjoying the benefits of meal prepping because it can be quite difficult to prepare their dishes especially when they are following a strict diet.

Meal prep can be different from one person to another. Hence it is important that you will find a schedule that will work well for you. The advantages of First, let me show you how meal prepping has become a life changer:

- **Saves time:** the main benefit of meal prepping is to save time. It enables you to eat healthy during the week without the hassle of preparing it for long hours. The truth is, it is hard to stare endlessly in front of your refrigerator not knowing what food to prepare for your family. With having effective meal prep, you can easily prepare meals in a jiffy plus it will lessen the time that you need to go to the supermarket just to buy your meal for the day.

- **Save money:** some people think that in order to eat healthy, you have to spend a great big amount of money. Meal prepping will prove them wrong! On the contrary, meal prepping will help save you some money because you will be able to buy bulk items and use your freezer as well. Do not be afraid to buy fresh herbs or big amounts of chicken. There are ways to store them for future use.

- **You will be able to multitask:** since you were able to save a lot of time prepping your meals, it allows you to do other tasks while cooking hence the reason why this system is perfect for people who are always on the go.

- **Allow you to make healthy food choices:** being busy does not give too much time for you to prepare meals at home, hence the reason why most of the time you opt for fast food meals. The good thing about meal prep is that you don't have to go through eating fast food meals every day. You don't need to rely on them as a last minute alternative.

- **Shopping is easier:** it helps you be organized and have a list of the things that you need to prepare your meals. Making a list will help avoid buying processed foods, and sugary products that you don't need.

- **Eliminates stress:** one of the greatest problems of busy individuals is making it home and preparing food for their family. It is stressful! With meal prepping, that will greatly change. Since you already have meals prepared in advance, food is served in a jiffy.

- **Learning portion control:** if you are following a strict diet or simply want to live a healthy life, portion control is equally important to be successful in your journey. Since you are already preparing for your meals in advance, you are able to know what food and how many calories are there in the food that you will be consuming. This will also give you a great insight on what foods are especially good for your health.

- **Adding variety in your meal:** though it may seem that meal prepping can be quite challenging, according to statistics people who are not planning for their meal have more tendencies to eat the same food over and over again. Meal prepping on the other hand, enables you to have a great deal of variety in your meals.

These are just some of the benefits that you can achieve once you start prepping ahead for your meals. The beauty about this is that there are no limits and no strict rules. You have the freedom to be creative and try out different meals for your whole family. The important thing is that you set aside a little time every week in order to do it. Once you get familiar with the system that works well with you, it would all happen in a breeze.

Chapter 2 – Let's get started

To assist you on how to get started, here are a few of the basic things you need to know so that you can plan and get prepped for your meals.

Evaluating your eating habits

You and your families' eating habits may change every week. It will all depend on your work schedule, school activities, travel plans, commitments and other schedule that you may have lined up for the week. Take a look at some of the situations you have to consider:

- How many meals a day? Assess the schedule that you and your family have. Have a rough idea on each and everyone's schedule so that you know how many meals you will be preparing for the week.

- The amount of time that you have to prepare: if you think that you really have a busy schedule during the week to come, consider looking for recipes that are easy to prepare or can be left out while you are working like slow cooker recipes.

- Your mood: food cravings, changes in season can greatly affect your meal prep. There may be times that the food you want to prepare do not have the ingredients available because it is out of season or unavailable. Weather conditions like winter or rainy seasons needs hot and warm food so try to be prepared for these kind of situation as well.

- Budget: think of produce that are on sale and in season. There are times that produce that are out of season can be a little expensive. So make sure that you have enough budget to carry out your meal preparations.

- Plan ahead by writing them down with the use of a pen and paper or your apps. Jot down your planned meals and for how many people would that be. Make sure that you also include what you can do with your leftovers.

Choosing your ingredients

Here are a couple of tips in choosing some of the fresh ingredients to prepare healthy and nutritious meals:

- *Look for local produce:* Depending on your location, it's best to know the local produce available in your market. That way, you will be able to plan the meals that you are going to prepare and you are already familiar with ingredients that are in season in your area.

- *Fish:* In choosing a whole fresh fish, make sure to check eyes for clarity. They should be crystal clear and is not sunken and cloudy. Make sure that the gills are bright red and not slimy. Poke the flesh and make sure that they will go back to their natural shape once you press them. If it doesn't go back to its natural shape, then it's no longer fresh. Smelling is also a key to know its freshness. Fresh fish smells like the smell of the ocean.

- *Meat:* Just like with fish, you would want to look for meat that is bright red in color. Avoid meat that already has a brownish red color. This means that it's no longer fresh. Make sure that you also smell your meat. If it smells bad, chances are, they are already there for quite a long time – don't buy it.

- *Chicken:* Fresh chicken should be pink in color. Do not buy chicken that is already grayish in color and has tears. Like meat and fish, it's important that they don't have a funky smell. So always make sure to smell them first. For frozen chicken, check for too much blood as they can be mishandled while packaging. This increases the risk of having a lot of bacterial contamination because they could have been thawed, then frozen a couple of times.

- *Carrots:* Choose carrots that are firm with smooth skin and bright orange in color. Make sure that they don't have any splits or damage and they are not pale, soft and have too many hairy roots. This shows signs of aging and is no longer fresh and crunchy.

- *Eggs:* Make sure that you check the expiration dates on every egg carton. Choose the batch that is recently delivered or newer. Do not buy eggs that smell bad and make sure that they are not chipped or have cracks. Once you get home, in my experience, I usually check them if they float or sink at the bottom of the water. Get a pot of water then place the eggs one by one. If the egg sinks and stays down, it's fresh. However, if the eggs float on top of the water, then they are no longer fresh and you should throw them away.

Just a rule of thumb in choosing fresh fruits and veggies, make sure that they don't have molds, holes, brown spots or wrinkled skin. Most fresh fruits and vegetables have vibrant colors, firm and plump. You can definitely differentiate them from the ones that are old and rotten.

Using your herbs and spices

Our food always tastes better when they are not under seasoned. However, you'll enjoy it a lot more if you know how to use herbs and spices. Be sure to season your prepped meals well to add pizzazz and great flavor!

- Herbs and spices are used to enhance the flavors of our food and not to hide or disguise them. Be selective in using your herb and spice combination. Do not use too many combinations as this would only confuse or change the taste of your dish.

- Do not season directly into your steaming pot. The moisture coming from the steaming pot may cause clumps or reduce the potency of the spice/herb that is left in the jar. This might also spoil them more quickly.

- For immediate release of flavor, crush herbs, like oregano, thyme, basil, in the palm of your hand before using it on your dish. This will wake up the flavors instantly.

- Dried herbs are used best when combined with oil or water because they will be infused a lot faster.

- Fresh herbs on the other hand provide full, bold flavor to your dish. This is also great for garnishing.

- Herbs like rosemary, thyme, sage, oregano and marjoram should be added to your dish early in the cooking process because the maximum flavor will be released during those stages. However, herbs that are delicate like cilantro, tarragon, parsley, basil and chives should be added at the last minute or else their flavors will get lost in the process.

Compiling your recipes

Since you are already set in prepping your meals, it's now time to take a look at various recipes that you will prepare. Look for those recipes that are nutritious, healthy and your family will surely enjoy. Create a master list where you can quickly find the recipe that you will prepare. Every time that you try one, be sure to add them on your roster of recipes.

Be creative and adventurous. Look for new recipes that are worth trying and take note of them. Make sure to take note of the nutrition facts so that you will be able to meet the necessary nutrients that you need especially if you are following a certain diet. Take a look at its serving portions as well since they are important in your meal prep. It will greatly help, especially if you will be feeding your whole family. Don't forget to plan on what you will do with the leftovers.

Another good thing about meal prepping is the use of ingredients. You can select recipes that have the same ingredients which help in minimizing the amount you need to buy. Finally, make that precious list before going to the grocery. Pick the schedule that would work well with your schedule and start prepping your meals.

Chapter 3 – Foods to Avoid and include

If you are already following a healthy diet, it is just okay to indulge once or even twice a week as long as you do not overdo it. Meal prepping is a great way to follow any diet, however there are some foods that can't be used to do some make ahead meals and foods that are best to make them.

Yes, you might think that these are just common sense, but hey, they are good reminders for you in order to have effective meal prep.

Here are the foods that are not good for meal prep:

- Heavily breaded foods
- Candies and cakes
- Deep fried foods
- Pastries
- Food that has refined sugars
- Foods that contain white flour and white flour for that matter
- All foods that have artificial sweeteners like Equal, Splenda, etc.
- Processed foods

- Foods that are rich in alcohol (except for special occasions)
- Boxed foods

Foods that you can include

- Whole grains like brown rice, quinoa, oats, wild rice
- Frozen or fresh berries
- Sweet potatoes
- Frozen or fresh veggies
- Legumes like dry beans
- Bread (whole wheat)
- Pasta (whole wheat)
- Low fat cheese
- Flour (whole wheat)
- Pastry flour (whole wheat)
- Yogurt (Greek, plain, low-fat, fat-free)
- Sorghum flour
- Dates
- Prunes raisins

Healthy fats and nuts you can include:

- EVOO or Extra Virgin Olive Oil
- Avocado
- Chia seeds
- Flax seeds
- Sunflower seeds
- Unrefined coconut oil
- Pumpkin seeds
- Walnuts, almonds, etc. (those that are not salty and have no added oil)

Condiments or Toppings

- Dijon mustard
- Salsa with no sugar added (if you are really on a strict weight loss diet)
- All natural cashew and almond butter
- Peanut butter (all natural)
- Sea salt
- Kosher salt

Lean protein

- Egg whites
- Eggs
- Lean meat
- Poultry
- Fish, especially salmon

Unrefined Sweeteners (to be used in moderation)

- Sorghum
- Molasses
- Honey
- Sucanat
- Maple syrup (100% pure)
- Stevia
- Palm sugar (coconut)

Oils and dressings

- Balsamic vinegar
- EVOO or Extra Virgin Olive Oil
- Red wine vinegar and others (without the added sugar, of course)

These are just some suggest foods and ingredients that you can add in making your food prep meal every day. As you go by becoming more and more familiar and acquainted with this type of habit, you can create new ingredient and be more bold on flavors and style. Have fun!

Chapter 4 – Useful tips and techniques

To fully enjoy the benefits of meal prep here are some useful tips and techniques that can guide you along the way.

Try out batch cooking

Batch cooking is preparing all or most of your meals for the whole week. All you need to do is provide at least an hour or two out of the day in the week. Just allot and schedule a day that you think would be convenient for you. There is no freezing necessary as you cook and eat the meals you've prepared throughout the week and this will simply go on a cycle.

Speed prepping techniques

Aside from learning how to batch cook, try following these useful techniques to speed up the preparation of your ingredients:

Using your kitchen scissors:

- To cut up the florets of cauliflower or broccoli
- To cut your meat into strips or cubes
- Or cut your herbs and other greens such as peppers, chives, green onions, etc.

Dice or chop potatoes ahead of time, then place them in your refrigerator for about 1-2 days. Make sure that they are soaked in water to avoid discoloration.

Use your food processor to prepare ingredients, especially if they are in bulk. It will not only save you time, but money as well. You food processor can help you:

- Chop or dice onions or celeries. Store them using a plastic bag in the refrigerator for about 1 to 2 days. If you freeze it, it will last for about a month.

- Shred cheese and freeze them in portions of 2 cups each. They can be stored up to 4 months in the freezer.

- Make bread crumbs. For faster and better bread crumb consistency, try freezing the bread first, then use the processor to make bread crumbs.

- Slice mushrooms and carrots. When storing the carrots, place it inside a plastic bag with moist paper towel to avoid becoming dry. Mushrooms should be kept in a well-ventilated container.

- Use your pizza cutter to cut bread and make them into croutons.

Storage tips

- Of course you can't store foods without efficient and safe containers. If you plan on doing this for a long time, make sure that you invest on good types of food storage such as mason jars, snapware, Tupperware, glass wares with lid, wax paper, foil or those that are simply BPA free. Remember that the food that you've prepared should be easily re-heated and these containers are the best for this purpose.

- Be sure that your containers are all in the same sizes so that they can be stacked neatly and easily as well.

- When storing food in the freezer, make sure that they are in small portions so that they can be thawed easily and those that you will only consume.

- Try to remove air as much as possible as it will cause freezer burn in your food. If you are using food containers put a parchment paper to reduce the amount of the air that come in direct contact with your food.

- Label food before freezing, so that you know what kind of food is stored.

- Make an inventory of what foods are available so that you won't have to make the same purchases. Also, be sure that they are dated properly so that you would know which ones to use first.

Pack them salads

Fruits and veggies are good for your health and including them in your weekly meal prep is also a great way to practice healthy eating. Here are some useful techniques to pack your greens and fruits.

When using plastic containers:

- Start first with the greens: to save time, try to use prewashed and pre-packed salad greens

- Add beans, fruits and veggies: make sure to dry off each of the ingredients before placing them in the container so that it is crispier longer.

- Add some protein: you can use grilled chicken, tofu, hard-boiled eggs, etc.

- Make sure that the dressings are separate until such time that you will be eating your salad.

When using mason jars:

- Use mason jars that are wide-mouthed as much as possible because they are easier to eat and fill out.

- Add first the salad dressing at the bottom. This is a great way of packing, especially if you don't have any separate container for the dressing.

- Add the veggies next. Start with the hard veggies like carrots, onions, radish, chickpeas, etc. Then follow it up with cherry tomatoes, bell peppers etc.

- Follow it up with the greens. This should occupy at least half of the jar. Make sure that they are dry.

- Place the proteins last.

- Shake the jar or pour the contents when ready to eat.

Suggested shopping lists for packing

- 2 pieces of avocados
- Sunflower seeds
- Mixed greens in large packages
- 2 pieces of cucumber
- 5 pieces of carrots
- A bag of grapes
- A package of cherry tomatoes
- A can of chickpeas
- 2 packs of tofu
- 2-3 pieces of bell pepper
- A bottle of your preferred salad dressings

Chapter 5 – Awesome Hacks and Ideas

To give you more ideas and tips on proceeding with your meal preparation, here are some awesome hacks you can definitely try out without having to push yourself too hard!

Cook once a week

Find a day where you can take up some time to do some grocery shopping. It would be nice to do some in bulk so you do not need to go back to the supermarket every now and then just to pick something up. This might seem like a time consuming task, but it would really save you a lot of time in the future.

So take a day or even a half to just buy the things you need for cooking then chop those vegetables and meat and get ready to cook. The advantage of this is that you only need to chop once a week, only need to preheat the oven once, and get everything ready. If it would take you around 10 minutes to cut everything you need for a meal, it would only take you about 40 to cut those you need for 5 meals, so why not do it all today and just keep them in the freezer where they would stay fresh for at least a week.

Not only is this a time saver, but definitely electricity saving as well, so you might as well consider committing yourself into cooking a batch of food once a week.

Keep it simple

No need to go and make super fancy, 5 star restaurant kind of dishes. Stay within your comfort zone and relax. Cooking is meant to be enjoyed. Do not make your life more complicated than it already is. Just keep it practical and find recipes that you would want to make and you think would enjoy making.

After all, you are trying to simplify your life by planning and preparing your meals ahead so why complicate it all by doing things that are way beyond your scope? Keep it real.

Take note of the food's timeline

Before you begin to mix and match your food, try to take note of the length of time it would stay fresh. Maybe you can post a note on your fridge door that tells you when the food you are going to eat are going to expire, or at least when to eat them best. This way, you would never waste food due to spoilage.

Also consider the quality of the food if you are planning to store it in the fridge for about a week or so. Consider the crispiness, the juiciness or the freshness of the food and take note of them.

Fill that freezer

Grab those freezer bags you have or maybe some Tupperware you can write on. Store your food in your fridge to keep them from going bad and remember to keep your fridge fool from time to time so that you do not go hungry and you are prepared for surprise guests that might come to your house.

Put that slow cooker into use

Maybe you are rushing things because you still want to go somewhere else. But keep in mind that cooking is not something to be done in a rush. It is something to be savored and loved. So why don't you put that slow cooker into use and cook some of the food you would like to see juicy, tender and delicious.

Slow cookers give you food that is just right to the taste, full of flavor and nutrition as well. Most food can even cook up to more than 8 hours so you can actually go to work and leave your cooker to finish cooking by itself.

Repeat your meals, all you want

No one is going to tell you that you ate that food last night like people tell you that they recognize what you wore yesterday. There is nothing wrong with repeating your food as much as you like. So just eat the one you like and repeat it as often as you want to.

You might want to remember your snacks

Meal preparing does not only have its scope on full-course meals, but also on those snacks you might want to try. Do not forget to include them in your meal preparation because as much as a beef steak is yummy, snacks leave you with a feeling of satisfaction you can only get by eating them.

You can always try some blueberries or grapes for a snack or some of your favorite sweets just so you have something to look forward to after you gobble your food down.

Mix and match

Be creative with your food, if you seem to be missing something, just look for something else to substitute it with. Cross-utilizing your ingredients are something that an innovative chef would do so try that one out. Think about the endless combinations of food you can create by doing so.

Spice it up

You already have an idea about your spices from the previous chapter so why not put them into action? Go find the right spice for the food you are cooking and brighten up its taste. Do not go for the normal looking dish and prepare a dish you are bound to love. Experimenting with food is always fun.

Keep your fridge organized

You know exactly how important your fridge is for you, so you must do your best to take care of it. Make some arrangement with your fridge and place it in a way that would be most convenient for you. Make it pleasing to the eyes and try to arrange it yourself so you would know exactly where anything is.

These are just some of the hacks that you can try out, but do not be bound by them. Along your journey through meal preparation, you are going to find out more hacks and maybe even create some of your own. The possibilities are endless and you only need to take the risk to achieve the things you want so good luck on preparing your meals!

Chapter 6 – Delicious Recipes

So now that you already have an idea on how to start with meal prepping, here are some great recipes you can follow and practice. These recipes are simply amazing and healthy. Go ahead and let's start prepping!

Breakfast

Buttermilk Pancakes

Ingredients

- A teaspoon of baking powder
- A pinch of salt
- A cup of all-purpose flour
- 1 beaten egg
- ½ teaspoon of baking soda
- A teaspoon of honey or raw sugar
- 1 ½ cups of buttermilk
- A tablespoon of melted butter

Directions

1. Combine baking powder, salt, baking soda and flour. Mix in the egg along with the buttermilk, then add it to the flour mixture. Stir well until it becomes smooth.

2. Add melted butter, then sugar.

3. Using a size ¼ measuring cup, scoop the batter, then fry on a griddle of about 325 to 350 degrees. This will make around 10 pancakes.

4. To store and freeze: cool it completely after it was cooked. Line a baking sheet using a parchment paper, then place the pancakes on it without touching one another. Add another layer of the parchment paper, then places another pancake until all pancakes are arranged and ready to be frozen.

5. Put it inside the refrigerator and freeze until it becomes solid. Once ready to use, you can heat it through toaster, microwave or griddle.

Breakfast Quesadillas

Ingredients

- A small diced red onions
- 2 tablespoons of olive oil (divided)
- Half cup of frozen or fresh corn kernels
- ½ teaspoon of ground cumin
- ½ teaspoon of salt (divided)
- A clove of minced garlic
- ¼ teaspoon of paprika (smoked)
- 8 large-sized eggs
- A pinch of black pepper
- A tablespoon of milk
- 10 pieces of large flour tortillas
- 1 (15 oz) canned black beans (rinsed and drained)
- ½ cup of salsa (chunky style; add 2 tablespoons more)
- 1 ½ cup of shredded cheese (depends on your preference)
- Greek yogurt, sliced avocado, chunky salsa (this is optional)

Directions

1. In a large-sized skillet, add a tablespoon of olive oil over a medium heat. Add onions and cook while stirring them occasionally for about 2 minutes. Add in the corn, cumin, ¼ teaspoon of salt, garlic and paprika. Cook for about 3-4 minutes, then transfer to a bowl. Set it aside.

2. Whisk together the milk, eggs and remaining pepper and salt. Place the skillet again over low to medium flame. Add the remaining tablespoon of olive oil. Once hot, add egg mixture and cook for around 3 to 4 minutes while stirring occasionally until it becomes scrambled. Remove from the heat.

3. Drain excess water from the bowl of veggie mixture if there are any. Add them in the skillet with the eggs. Add in the black beans the combine well. Season to taste.

4. In your working station, place a tortilla and spoon about 1/10 of egg mixture on the half side of the tortilla, make sure that you leave a small space to allow folding.

5. Top it with cheese and a tablespoon of salsa, then fold the empty half on top of the filling. This should look like a semi-circle. Repeat the same process on the remaining tortilla.

6. To cook, add a small amount of oil or cooking spray on a non-stick pan. Place the prepared tortilla and cook around 5 to 6 minutes until both of the sides are browned and cheese melted. Repeat until all tortillas are cooked.

7. Cut into triangles, then serve hot. This will make 10 quesadillas.

8. For make-ahead meals: cook the eggs and veggies as directed then let cool. Assemble them in the same way, but instead of cooking, wrap each of the quesadilla using a plastic wrap. To prevent it from bending, place them in a container with a flat surface. Put inside the freezer until it becomes firm. Once firm, transfer in an airtight container, then store it back to the freezer.

9. Once you are ready to eat them, remove plastic wrap, warm in a microwave for about 2-3 minutes until it is thoroughly heated. Another way of heating it is to thaw them first, then cook in the skillet as mentioned in the recipe.

Berry-Berry Blue Breakfast Bars

Ingredients

- 1 ½ cup of 100% pure rolled oats
- ¾ cups of almonds (whole)
- ½ cup of blueberries (dried)
- ½ cup of pistachios
- 1/3 cup of flaxseed (ground)
- 1/3 of walnuts
- 1/3 cup of pepitas
- ¼ cup of sunflower seeds
- 1/3 cup of pure honey (you can also use maple syrup)
- ¼ cup of apple sauce (unsweetened)
- 1 cup of almond butter

Directions

1. Place wax or parchment paper in an 8x8 baking pan, leaving the paper hang over the edges.
2. Combine rolled oats, almonds, blueberries, pistachios, flaxseed, walnuts, pepitas and sunflower seeds in a large sized bowl and mix them all together.

3. Slowly add the honey and continue to lightly stir. Then add the almond butter and mix them well.

4. Place the batter mix in the lined baking pan and press it firmly using the palm of your hands or if you have a mini roller, you can use that as well. Make sure that it's evenly distributed and rolled.

5. Freeze for about an hour. Remove from the freezer and slowly lift the paper with the portion of the mixture. Gently peel the paper and slice it diagonally to long bars, this would make at least 8 bars. Cut them in half to create 16 bars. Place them on a reseal-able bag and put them in the freezer.

6. When you are in a hurry, just get a piece and voila! Enjoy! Makes 16 delicious bars.

Lunch

Chicken and Garlic Lime Kebabs

Ingredients

- ¼ cup of EVOO (extra virgin olive oil)
- 2 cloves of minced garlic
- A teaspoon of pepper
- A teaspoon of salt
- 4 chicken breasts (boneless and skinless, cut to 1 ½ inch)
- 1 piece of lime (juiced)
- 1-2 teaspoons of Sriracha (if desired)
- Skewers

Directions

1. Combine lime juice, EVOO, pepper, salt, garlic and Sriracha. Pour over chicken and place it in a Ziploc or resealable bag. Marinate for about 2-8 hours in the refrigerator.
2. Remove the chicken and thread it on the skewers.
3. Preheat your grill to medium to high heat.

4. Cook chicken for about 10 to 15 minutes. Turn on once in awhile until chicken is cooked fully.

5. To store, place the raw chicken in the freezer. Make sure that your resealable bag is freezer safe. Once ready to cook, thaw first. Serves 4.

Veggie Taco Salad

Ingredients

For the cilantro and lime dressing

- Juice from a lime
- ½ cup of loosely packed fresh cilantro
- A tablespoon of apple cider vinegar
- A teaspoon of honey
- A pinch of salt
- ¼ cup of Greek yogurt (non-fat and plain)

For the salad

- ½ cup of black beans
- ¼ diced cucumber
- ¼ cup of corn
- 3 cups of mixed greens
- 1 piece of diced Roma tomato
- ¼ cup of diced red pepper
- A tablespoon of cheddar cheese (shredded)

- ¼ of diced avocado

Directions

1. Prepare the salad dressing by blending the ingredients all together. Pour it in the bottom of your mason jar, about a quart size. Use those wide-mouth jars)

2. Layer the ingredients in this order: cucumber, black beans, then tomato, corn, then the red pepper, mixed greens, avocado and the cheese.

3. Cap it tightly with the lid and place in the refrigerator. This can be stored for 5 days. You can also choose to crush a few tortilla chips on top when you eat it. Enjoy! Serves: 1

Baked Fish Sticks

Ingredients

- 1/3 cup of EVOO
- 3 pieces of large eggs
- 3 cups of Panko bread crumbs
- A tablespoon of seafood seasoning
- 2 ½ lbs of tilapia fillets (skinless and cut to an inch strips)
- Kosher salt
- Ketchup and coleslaw to serve

Directions

1. Preheat your oven to 450 degrees F. Using a large-sized rimmed baking pan, place the bread crumbs along with the seafood seasoning, half a teaspoon of salt and oil. Toast inside the oven, tossing it once, for about 5-7 minutes or until it becomes golden brown. Transfer to a bowl.

2. Meanwhile, beat eggs with a tablespoon of water. Dip the fish in the eggs and coat it with the toasted bread crumbs. Shake excess crumbs, then place it on a baking pan lined with parchment paper.

3. Bake for about 12-15 minutes or until opaque and crispy. Serve it with ketchup or coleslaw if you like.

4. Uncooked fish stocks can be frozen and stored until 3 months. Freeze them first on a baking sheet until it becomes firm. Transfer to freezer bags and keep in refrigerator. Once you are ready to cook, bake frozen for about 18-20 minutes. Serves 8.

Veggie and Grilled Chicken Bowls

Ingredients

- 16 oz of cooked quinoa
- 4 cups of chopped roasted asparagus
- 4 cups of cauliflower (roasted)
- 4 cups of broccoli florets (roasted)
- 16 oz of cooked brown rice

You can also replace the veggies with:

- 4 cups of Brussels sprouts (roasted)
- 4 cups of haricot verts

For the grilled chicken

- A teaspoon of kosher salt
- A teaspoon of ground cumin
- ½ teaspoon of garlic salt
- ½ teaspoon of smoked paprika
- ½ teaspoon of ground pepper

- 2 pieces of lime
- 3-4 pieces of medium sized chicken breasts (boneless)

Directions

1. To prepare the chicken: preheat your grill. Combine pepper, salt, paprika, cumin and the garlic salt in a bowl. Pour them over the chicken and place it inside a Ziploc or resealable bag. Squeeze the juice of lime inside and marinade for about 1 to 5 hours. You can also grill it immediately. Spray some cooking spray on the grill and cook chicken for about 5 to 6 minutes on each side or until chicken is cooked thoroughly. Let rest for about 10 minutes. Slice chicken thinly and squeeze some more lime juice on top of the chicken.

2. To prepare your veggie bowls, get containers that have the same size. Place ¼ cup of quinoa and rice on each of the container. Top it with 1 ½ cups of roasted veggies, then add in about ½ cup of sliced chicken. Store in the refrigerator and reheat when ready to eat. You can add in a low-fat dressing, salsa or hot sauce of choice once heated. Serves 8.

3. In roasting your veggies, place on a large sized baking sheet, then drizzle it with EVOO and season to taste with pepper and salt. Cook in your oven over a 375 degrees F until it becomes tender.

Dinner

Orange Chicken

Ingredients

- Juice of 3 oranges
- 3 tablespoons of fat, preferably coconut oil
- 1 teaspoon of fresh ginger
- Zest from 1 orange
- 1 teaspoon of chili garlic sauce
- 3 tablespoons of coconut aminos, Note: you can substitute with wheat-free soy sauce
- 1 pound of chicken breast, already cut into bite size pieces

Directions

1. Combine the zest, orange juice, coconut aminos, ginger, and chili garlic sauce in medium size sauce pot over medium heat. Let it simmer for a while.

2. While letting the first ingredients to simmer, heat 3 tablespoon of fat in a sauté pan over medium high heat. Add all the chicken breast and let it cook until the color becomes brown and a crust has already formed in each chicken piece.

3. You can now add the chicken in the sauce pot you have prepared a while ago and stir in order for it to absorb the orange goodness of the orange sauce. Serve and enjoy!

4. You can also let it cool down for a while (at least for 30 minutes) and then preserve it in the freezer. Just reheat in the oven if you are now ready to eat. Serves 4-6.

5. Note: if you are not satisfied with the orange taste, try adding more zest until the desired flavor is attained.

Burrito Bowl

Ingredients

For quinoa:

- 2 cups of water
- ½ teaspoon of salt
- 1/4cup of fresh cilantro (chopped)
- Zest and juice of a lime
- A cup of quinoa

For chicken

- 2 teaspoons of sea salt
- 2 pieces of large-sized chicken
- A tablespoon of ghee or coconut oil

Other ingredients

- 2 pieces of bacon (if desired)
- A large sized sweet potato (washed and cut to half an inch cube)
- A tablespoon of bacon fat (you can also use coconut oil)

- ¾ cup of shredded cheese
- 5 tablespoons of Greek yogurt (plain)
- 3 cups of chopped lettuce
- ½ cup of fresh cilantro

Directions

1. To prepare the quinoa: add water, salt and quinoa in a pot and bring to boil. Cook and cover for about 20 to 25 minutes or until it becomes fluffy and soft. Let cool and set aside. Once cooled, add lime juice and zest, then the ¼ cup of cilantro. Stir to combine well. Add additional lime and adjust taste according to liking.

2. To prepare the chicken: pat dry the chicken breast and season each side with salt. Using a large-sized pan, heat ghee over medium to high heat. Cook chicken around 4 minutes on each of its sides or until it becomes brown. Let cool and cut chicken into small chunks. Set aside.

3. Cook the bacon until crispy. Reserve the oil and use it to cook the sweet potatoes. Sear and stir every 3 to 5 minutes. Turn heat to low and continue cooking sweet potatoes until it becomes fork tender. Cool and set aside.

4. To assemble your burrito bowl: once all of the ingredients are cooled, add a tablespoon of Greek yogurt at the bottom of the jar. Top it with around 2 tablespoons of cooked sweet potatoes. Then top it with 3

to 4 tablespoons of the quinoa mixture and layer it with cheese, then a little of crumbled bacon then chicken. Fill it up with salad greens and top it with chopped cilantro before closing lid. Can make at least 5 salad jars.

Freezer-Friendly meatballs

This recipe can make for up to 30 medium sized meatballs.

Ingredients

- 1 sprig fresh rosemary, minced
- 2 garlic cloves, minced
- 1 long sprig fresh oregano, minced
- 3 sprigs fresh thyme, minced
- ½ small yellow onion, already chopped
- ¼ cup flat leaf parsley, already chopped
- 2 medium sized eggs, already whisked
- ½ cup of almond meal
- Black pepper
- 1 teaspoon of red pepper flakes
- ½ cup of Parmesan, already finely shredded
- ¼ cup of cream, Note: this is optional.
- ¼ cup of bacon fat
- 1 pound of ground beef

Directions

1. In a medium sized bowl mixed all the ingredients (except the bacon fat) until they are all combined. Using your bare hands, roll and make meatballs. Tip: you can freely roll them into your desired sized, but is much better to make them medium in size in order to cook better.

2. Over medium to medium-high heat, heat the bacon fat in a sauté pan and wait until it's hot enough. You can now add the meatballs and let them fry for about 7 minutes or wait until the bottom is already brown in color.

3. After cooking on one side, turn the meatballs on the opposite side in order for the other side to cook. Wait until that side is also browned. This will take for about another 7 minutes. Put the meatballs in a plate after being cooked. Serve and enjoy! And of course, let the others cool down first and freeze them for you, eat them on any other day.

4. You can cut one meatball in the center and see if it's fully cooked on the inside. If not, just turn the heat to low and let it stay for a few more minutes. It's also inevitable that you'll be able to make many meatball pieces and you can't cook them all at once. The trick is to cook them in batches and the put the cooked batches in a warm oven (to keep it hot) while the other batch is being fried. This recipe makes about 30 meatballs.

Fennel and Sausage Ragu

Ingredients

- 6 cloves of garlic (minced)
- 2 small white onions (diced)
- 2 small fennel bulbs (diced)
- 2 (32 oz) diced tomatoes, include its juices
- 1 (15 oz) canned tomato puree
- A pound of hot Italian sausage
- EVOO
- 1 sprig of rosemary
- Pepper and salt to taste
- Cooked pasta (for serving)
- Grated Parmesan cheese (for serving)

Directions

1. Crumble and sauté sausage with olive oil using a deep pan or Dutch oven. Brown sausage for around 10-15 minutes and continue to stir and scrape. Don't worry if it sticks at the bottom of the pan. It will be used as you cook along the way.

2. Add the diced onions, fennel and minced garlic. Stir well to combine the sausage with the veggies. Turn the heat down and cook veggies with sausage for about 15 minutes. Once the veggies are tender, add canned tomatoes and tomato puree. Stir and simmer on low to medium heat. Add salt, black pepper and the rosemary sprig. Continue simmering and loosely cover the pan. Take off the lid after an hour and adjust taste according to your liking.

3. Ladle a good amount of ragu over your cooked pasta and sprinkle it with cheese and fennel fronds on top. You can refrigerate this ragu for about 5 days and keep frozen for a few months. Makes about 8 servings

Stir-Fry Frozen Dinners

Ingredients

For the base to be stir-fried:

- A pound of chicken thigh or breast (you can also use other proteins such as tofu, beef or pork)
- ½ cup of uncooked brown or white rice
- 2 cloves of smashed garlic
- 1 bell pepper (chopped)
- A cup of sugar snap peas (you can also use other veggies)

For the sauce

- 2 tablespoons of dry sherry
- 2 tablespoons of soy sauce
- 2 tablespoons of water (you can also use veggie or chicken broth)
- A tablespoon of vinegar (rice wine)
- A teaspoon of sesame oil
- A teaspoon of cornstarch (if you want to have thicker sauce)

Directions

1. Prepare rice according to the directions on the package. Once done, spread rice over a baking pan and let cool. Transfer using a container or freezer bag. Refrigerate and set aside.

2. Add chicken, bay leaf and garlic on a pit. Add water to make sure that the chicken is covered with a few inches of water. Poach and cook chicken on medium to high heat. Let it boil. Once boiling, lower the heat, then cover the pot and continue to cook for about 10-13 minutes or until chicken is cooked through. If you are using tofu, it does not need to be pre-cooked.

3. Once chicken is cooked, cut into uniform slices and transfer on a baking sheet lined with parchment paper. Make sure to leave room for the veggies.

4. Cut the veggies with the same size as the chicken, then place them beside the chicken. Freeze chicken and veggies until it becomes solid for about 4 hours. You can also do it overnight. Once frozen solid, pack them into freezer bags and make sure to press out air as much as possible.

5. Prepare the sauce by whisking together all of the ingredients. Pour them in a freezer bag and be sure that bags don't have leaks or holes. Again, make sure to press out air as much as possible.

6. Pack all the ingredients together: the rice, sauce, chicken and veggies, on a large sized freezer bag or

container. Label them accordingly and seal it without too much air as possible. They can be stored until 3 months. This serves 2.

7. To heat your stir-fry meal: defrost the sauce first. Transfer rice in a microwaveable container which is covered loosely and heat for around 2 minutes. You can also incorporate the rice while cooking the chicken and veggies in the wok.

8. Meanwhile, add 2 teaspoons of oil in a large-sized pan. Add chicken and cook for about 4-6 minutes. Add veggies and cook. Stir occasionally until it is warmed through and crisp tender. Mix the sauce and stir fry until sauce thickens. Serve on top of the rice. Enjoy!

Snacks

Mini Parfaits

Ingredients

- 5 teaspoons of honey (clover)
- 1 ¼ cups of Greek yogurt (vanilla)
- 1 ¼ cups of frozen berries
- 5 tablespoons or more of your preferred granola mix
- Mason jars

Directions

1. Divide all the ingredients equally on 5 (4 oz) mason jars. Place the fruit first on the bottom, then honey, the granola mix and finish it up with yogurt. Cover with the lid and store in the refrigerator. This can last for around 3-5 days.

Healthy Snack Bin

Ingredients

- Baby carrots
- Red grapes
- Strawberries
- String cheese
- Apples
- Trail mix of your choice

Directions

1. Place all the ingredients on different packages. To keep the berries fresh, rinse them with a water and vinegar mixture, 1 part vinegar (either apple cider or white) and 10 parts of water. Then place on a freezer package. Store in the refrigerator until ready to consume. The amount of these snack bins will depend on how much you want to prepare and how long you want it to last.

Nuts and Seeds Granola Bar

Ingredients

- 1 cup of walnuts (raw)
- 1 ½ cups of almonds (raw)
- 1 cup of pumpkin seeds (raw or sprouted)
- ½ cup of sesame and flax seed combo
- 1 cup of shredded coconut (unsweetened)
- 1 teaspoon of cinnamon
- 2 tablespoons of water
- 3 tablespoons of coconut oil
- 1 teaspoon of vanilla extract
- ½ teaspoon of cinnamon (ground)
- ½ teaspoon of kosher salt
- 1 egg (beaten lightly)

Directions

1. Preheat your oven to 300 degrees.
2. Line your baking tray using a parchment paper.
3. Place the walnuts, almonds and pumpkin seeds in the blender or food processor. Pulse a few times until it becomes finely chopped. Makes sure not to grind them into a fine texture.
4. In a large sized mixing bowl, whisk egg white with water until it becomes bubbly and a bit foamy. Add vanilla extract, salt and cinnamon and whisk well.
5. Pour in the chopped nuts and seeds together with the shredded coconut. Mix well until everything is evenly coated.
6. Spread the mixture evenly on the lined baking pan. Bake for around 40 minutes or until it becomes crispy and golden brown. Stir it twice.
7. Remove from the oven and allow to cool for about 10 minutes. Using your spatula, scrape the granola and

release the large clusters. Once cooled, store it in a resealable plastic or airtight glass jar.
8. Serve it on top of coconut yogurt with fruits or you can add dried fruit. Enjoy!

Spicy Jicama Shoestring Fries

Ingredients:

- 1 piece of large Jicama (spiraled into noodles)
- 2 tablespoons of olive oil for drizzling
- Pinch of salt to taste
- 1 tablespoon of powdered onion
- 2 tablespoons of cayenne pepper
- 2 tablespoons of powdered chili

Directions

1. Preheat your oven to 405 degrees.
2. Place your Jicama noodles on a baking tray and cut them into small sized noodles making them look like shoestring fries.
3. Drizzle them with olive oil and lightly toss to evenly coat the noodles.
4. Season the Jicama noodles with salt, cayenne pepper, powdered onion and powdered chili. Again lightly toss them so that the spices and seasoning will be evenly distributed. Make sure not to overcrowd the noodles to avoid sticking together.
5. Bake for 15 minutes, then turns it over to bake them again for another 10 to minutes or until your preferred crispiness.
6. Store in an airtight container until 3 days.

Slow cooker recipes

The use of a slow cooker is another great way to practice make-ahead meals or meal prep. Not only are they easy because you will simply put them all in one pot and let them cook, it's one of the best ways to make delicious meals and save time. Here are some great slow cooker recipes for you to enjoy!

Breakfast Porridge

Ingredients

- ½ cup of wild or red rice
- ½ cup of oats (choose the steel-cut ones)
- ¼ cup of faro or pearl barley
- ½ cup of wheat cereal or farina
- 1 piece of orange peel (cut to 2 inch slices)
- 1 piece of cinnamon stick
- 1-2 tablespoons of brown sugar (choose from dark or light color)
- ¼ teaspoon of salt
- ¼ cup of dried fruit (choose your favorite fruits)
- 5 cups of water
- Chopped nuts, milk or maple syrup to serve (optional)

Directions

1. 12 hours before serving, you can prepare this dish in time for breakfast. Place rice, barley, farina and oats inside the slow cooker. Mix in cinnamon stick, salt, sugar, 5 cups of water and orange peel. Add also the dried fruit of your choice.
2. Set the slow cooker for the porridge cycle, such that it will be cooked and prepared once you wake up in the morning. If you don't have a porridge cycle, you can cook for about an hour and warm them in the morning.
3. Serve with syrup or milk, top with nuts if you prefer. Enjoy!
4. Serves 4-6

Breakfast Casserole

Ingredients

- A bag of 32 ounces of hash brown potatoes (frozen)
- 1 pound of bacon
- 1 piece diced small onion
- 8 ounces of cheddar cheese, sharp (shredded)
- ½ of diced bell pepper (red)
- ½ of diced bell pepper (green)
- 12 eggs
- 1 cup of milk

Directions

1. Slice bacon into small pieces and cook well. Drain excess fat.
2. Add half a bag of hash browns at the bottom of the crockpot, then add half of the cooked bacon, half onions, half of the red and green bell peppers and shredded cheese.
3. Place remaining half of hash browns on top. Followed by the remaining bacon, onions, cheese and the red and green bell peppers.
4. Meanwhile, crack 12 eggs in a bowl and whisk together with the milk. Pour this mixture inside the crockpot and add pepper and salt.
5. Cook the mixture for 4 hours on low.
6. Serve hot and enjoy! Serves 4-5.

Easy Pea-sy Soup

Ingredients

- ½ cup of fresh parsley (chopped; plus add 8-10 parsley stems more)
- 4 sprigs of thyme
- 1 pound of green split peas (rinsed and picked over)
- 1 large sized leek (use the light green and white part only; halved and sliced thinly)
- 2 stalks of chopped celery
- 2 pieces of carrots (chopped)
- Salt and pepper
- 1 smoked leg of turkey (around 1 to 1 ½ pounds)
- ¼ cup of plain yogurt (non-fat)
- ½ cup of frozen peas (thawed)
- Crusty bread to serve (optional)

Directions

1. Tie thyme together with parsley stems using a kitchen string. Place it in the slow cooker. Add leek, split peas, carrots, celery, a teaspoon of salt and half a teaspoon of pepper. Mix them to combine. Add turkey leg plus 7 cups of water, then cover.
2. Cook on low for about 6-8 hours or until peas and turkey are tender. Once done, discard the twigs of herb. Discard bone and skin from the turkey, then shred its meat.
3. Stir the soup vigorously to break peas and make soup smoother. You can add water if it is too thick for your preference.
4. Add about ¾ of the shredded turkey to the soup. Set aside a few meats for garnishing. Add chopped parsley and season with pepper and salt.

5. Ladle soup on serving bowls. Top with thawed green peas and meat. Serve with bread if you want. Enjoy! Serves 1.

Chicken with Gravy Slow Cooker style

Ingredients

- 4-5 lbs of whole chicken
- 2 tablespoons ghee
- 2 medium sized onions (chopped)
- 6 cloves peeled garlic
- 1 teaspoon of tomato paste
- ¼ cup of chicken stock
- ¼ cup of white wine
- Your favorite seasoning
- Kosher salt
- Fresh ground pepper

Directions

1. Prepare and chop all your vegetables.
2. Using a large sized cast iron pan, melt ghee over medium to high heat. Sauté garlic and the onions. Add tomato paste. Cook for about 8-10 minutes and season the veggies with pepper and salt.
3. When all the veggies are lightly brown and soft, deglaze pan with white wine and transfer everything in your slow cooker.
4. Meanwhile, season your chicken with pepper and salt and your favorite seasoning. Make sure to season them inside and out. Place the chicken, breast facing down inside the cooker. Cook on low heat for about 4-6 hours.
5. Once the cooking is done, take the chicken out and let it sit for about 20 minutes.
6. Take the excess fat on top of the vegetables in the slow cooker. Using an immersion blender or hand blender, blend thoroughly until mixture turned to mouth-watering gravy. Adjust seasoning according to preference.

7. Slice or rip off your chicken using your hands (this is pretty much exciting!). Place on a serving plate and put gravy on top or a small bowl.
8. Eat up and enjoy!

Vegetarian Lasagna

Ingredients

- 1 26 oz jar of marinara sauce
- 1 14 ½ oz of canned diced tomatoes
- 1 8 oz pack of no-boil lasagna noodles
- 1 15 oz container of part-skimmed ricotta cheese
- 1 8 oz pack of mozzarella (shredded)
- 1 10 oz pack of frozen spinach (thawed, chopped and squeezed to dry)
- 1 cup of veggie crumbles (frozen)

Directions

1. In a medium-sized bowl, combine tomatoes with its juice and marinara sauce.
2. Meanwhile, using a non-stick cooking spray, spray the bottom of the crockpot. Spoon a cup of tomato sauce mixture at the bottom.
3. Arrange ¼ of the noodles over the sauce. Overlap the noodles and make sure to break them in order to cover much of the sauce.
4. Spoon about ¾ cup of sauce on top of the noodles and top it with a half a cup of ricotta and half a cup of shredded mozzarella. Spread half of the spinach on top of the cheese.
5. Repeat doing the same process, twice beginning with the noodles. Once in the middle layer, replace the spinach using the frozen crumbles. Put remaining noodles and top it with the remaining sauce and cheese.

6. Cover and cook for about 2 ½ - 3 hours on low while 1 ½ - 2 hours on high or you can check to see if the noodles are already tender.
7. Serve hot and enjoy!

Smoothies

Another fantastic idea for meal prepping is using them for smoothies. Prep the ingredients ahead of time and make your very own smoothie. You can place them in a freezer prep jar so that you easily blend them and take them with you.

Energizing Superfood Smoothie

Ingredients

- ½ of avocado

- 1 cup of coconut water

- ½ cup of kale

- ½ cup of tropical fruit (papaya, mango, pineapple or combination)

- ½ cup of spinach

- 1/3 cup of Greek yogurt

- 2 tablespoons of goji berries

- 2 tablespoons of cranberries (dried)

- 1 teaspoon of coconut oil

- 1 teaspoon of Maca

- 1 tablespoon of coconut flakes

- 1 teaspoon of wheatgrass powder

- Sweeteners (this is optional; choose from honey, stevia or maple syrup)

Directions

Place all of the ingredients in your blender. Blend well until smooth. Transfer to a glass and enjoy!

Banana, Spinach and Strawberry

Ingredients

- 2 cups of baby spinach
- 1 large sized banana
- A cup of water
- 4 large sliced strawberries

Directions

Place all of the ingredients in your blender. Blend well until smooth. Transfer to a glass and enjoy!

Kiwi and Banana Smoothie

Ingredients

- ½ cup of water
- 1 medium sized banana (frozen or fresh)
- A cup of baby spinach
- 2 pieces of kiwi (cut in half and peeled)
- Sea salt
- ½ tablespoon of coconut oil
- A tablespoon of flax seeds or Chia seeds
- A tablespoon of coconut flakes or shreds
- Sweeteners like maple syrup, honey or stevia (if desired)

Directions

Place all of the ingredients in your blender. Blend well until smooth. Transfer to a glass and enjoy!

Banana Superfood Smoothie

Ingredients

- 1 medium sized banana (frozen or fresh)
- A cup of spinach
- 1 ½ cups of almond milk
- ½ cup of strawberries (frozen or fresh)
- 2 tablespoons of Greek yogurt
- ½ cup of mango chunks (frozen or fresh)
- A tablespoon of coconut oil
- A tablespoon of bee pollen
- A tablespoon of Chia seed gel or Chia seeds
- A cup of kale
- 1 tablespoon of gelatin (you can also use your own protein powder)
- 1 tablespoon of hemp seeds
- Any other Superfoods that you have (optional)

Directions

Place all of the ingredients in your blender. Blend well until smooth. Transfer to a glass and enjoy!

Orange and Carrot Smoothie

Ingredients

- 2 pieces of peeled clementines
- 4 pieces of shredded carrots (this should be about 2 cups)
- 2/3 cup of Greek yogurt (vanilla)
- A cup of romaine lettuce (chopped)
- ½ cup of ice cubes

Directions

Place all of the ingredients in your blender. Blend well until smooth. Transfer to a glass and enjoy!

Fruity Power Smoothie

Ingredients

- 2 cups of watermelon (cubed and seeded, rinds removed)
- 1 ½ cups of frozen strawberries (unsweetened)
- 1 ½ cup of small-sized cauliflower (florets only)
- 1 (6 oz) Greek yogurt (strawberry flavored)
- 2 tablespoons of strawberry preserves (if desired)

Directions

1. Using a small-sized saucepan, cook the cauliflower for around 10 minutes or till it becomes very tender. Drain, then rinse with cold water.

2. Place the cooked cauliflower, strawberries, yogurt, watermelon and strawberry preserves if you will use it. Cover then blend until smooth. Pour in a tall glass. Serve and enjoy!

Conclusion

You have reached the final page of this book. I hope you have learned so much from this book and eventually make it a habit of your own. You see how wonderful meal prepping is? Take your time and be not afraid to start little by little. Remember that you don't have to prep it all. If you are just a beginner, this will definitely be overwhelming for you. Make sure that you try it to prepare your meals better for just a day or two. Don't do it all for one week. Once you get comfortable with the process, everything will be easy breezy.

Another reminder is to follow recipes first, especially those that you already familiar with. This will help in giving you confidence as you go along your meal prep habit. Just focus on preparing the meals ahead of time. Make this book as your guide in your prepping habit. Enjoy and include your family members as well, especially your children. This will help them learn the basics at an early age and teach them how to eat healthily.

Finally, give yourself some time to get used to this process. Remember, nothing is learned overnight. There will definitely be some mishaps and mistakes, but over time you will learn from them. Do not get discouraged if that happens. Take note that meal prep is about making it easier for you and provide your family a healthy meal every day. Not make it stressful for you. So just take it easy. I am confident that you will be able to push through and be successful in this journey.

Again, thank you and have a healthy and happy meal prep journey!
*-- **George Walton***

Copyright 2016 by George Walton - All rights reserved

This document is geared towards providing exact and reliable information in regards to the topic and issue covered. The publication is sold with the idea that the publisher is not required to render accounting, officially permitted, or otherwise, qualified services. If advice is necessary, legal or professional, a practiced individual in the profession should be ordered.

- From a Declaration of Principles which was accepted and approved equally by a Committee of the American Bar Association and a Committee of Publishers and Associations.

In no way is it legal to reproduce, duplicate, or transmit any part of this document in either electronic means or in printed format. Recording of this publication is strictly prohibited and any storage of this document is not allowed unless with written permission from the publisher. All rights reserved.

The information provided herein is stated to be truthful and consistent, in that any liability, in terms of inattention or otherwise, by any usage or abuse of any policies, processes, or directions contained within is the solitary and utter responsibility of the recipient reader. Under no circumstances will any legal responsibility or blame be held against the publisher for any reparation, damages, or monetary loss due to the information herein, either directly or indirectly.

Respective authors own all copyrights not held by the publisher.

The information herein is offered for informational purposes solely, and is universal as so. The presentation of the information is without contract or any type of guarantee assurance.

The trademarks that are used are without any consent, and the publication of the trademark is without permission or backing by the trademark owner. All trademarks and brands within this book are for clarifying purposes only and are the owned by the owners themselves, not affiliated with this document.

CPSIA information can be obtained
at www.ICGtesting.com
Printed in the USA
LVOW13s0757020117
519404LV00019B/1624/P